GROWING TOGETHER IN

GRATITUDE

GROWING TOGETHER IN

GRATITUDE

CHARACTER STORIES FOR FAMILIES

FAMILYLIFE®

Little Rock, Arkansas

BARBARA RAINEY

GROWING TOGETHER IN GRATITUDE

FamilyLife Publishing®

5800 Ranch Drive

Little Rock, Arkansas 72223

1-800-FL-TODAY • FamilyLife.com

FLTI, d/b/a FamilyLife®, a ministry of Campus Crusade for Christ International®

Unless otherwise noted, Scripture quotations are taken from the New American Standard Bible®, Copyright © 1960, 1962, 1963, 1968, 1971, 1972, 1973, 1975, 1977, 1995 by The Lockman Foundation. Used by permission. (www.Lockman.org)

Scripture quotations marked (NIV) are taken from the New International Version®. Copyright © 1973, 1978, 1984 by Biblica. Used by permission of Zondervan. All rights reserved.

ISBN: 978-1-60200-397-2

Design: Brand Navigation, LLC

Printed in the United States of America

2010—Second Edition

14 13 12 11 10   1 2 3 4 5

Help for today. Hope for tomorrow.

dedicated to

Samuel Escue

May you always be grateful
Every day and in every way
For all that God brings and all that he withholds.
His love surrounds you;
His will is always good.
Remember him.
Honor him.
And with a thankful heart,
May you lead others to see Jesus in you
All the days of your life.

CONTENTS

WHY GRATITUDE

One of my greatest discouragements as a mom was my children's complaining and griping. It was an ongoing dilemma that often left me downcast. Why couldn't they be thankful for their food rather than complain about the vegetables they had to eat or where they had to sit at the table? In an effort to combat this irritating tendency, we memorized some verses as a family and encouraged our six children to focus on the positives rather than the negatives. But ultimately, being grateful is a choice involving the will. Parents can coach and direct their children to express gratitude, but the heart of a child cannot be controlled.

The same is true for us as adults, isn't it?

If we're honest, we aren't always thankful for our lot in life. Being grateful, for those who are believers in Christ, is an expression of the depth of our trust in God. If he is our Father, our Parent, our response to him should be better than our children's immature responses to us, right?

We often struggle with being thankful because we have so much today, and we feel we deserve it. We're selfish and want what we want. And because we're often disappointed, we feel that being thankful applies only to the good times. But God has made it clear in his Word that expressing gratitude is not optional. He has commanded us multiple times to give thanks to him—for example, "Always [give] thanks for all things in the name of our Lord Jesus Christ to God, even the Father" (Ephesians 5:20). There are no exception clauses in that command.

The story of how God dealt with the people of Israel and their grumbling has always encouraged me as a parent to continually train my kids in gratitude. (The story is found

IS IMPORTANT

in Numbers 13–14 and is referenced later in 1 Corinthians 10.) The nation of Israel didn't believe that God would deliver them as he promised, and instead of choosing faith, they chose fear. These men and women gave in to their emotions and grumbled, complained, and cried. (Sounds a lot like what my children did at times.) God's discipline was to make them wander in the wilderness for forty years! I may have made my children sit on their bed for thirty minutes . . . but not forty years! Obviously, God takes a lack of faith, expressed in a complaining attitude, very seriously. Perhaps we should too.

How do parents develop an attitude of gratitude in their children? It's not easy and won't happen quickly, but I believe that inspiring our children with role models is one way to help them choose to be grateful. By giving them heroes to look up to, we guide their hearts with memories of others who made good choices. We can motivate our children to follow those who have lived nobly.

Choosing gratitude is an act of belief because it always involves a denial of self for the higher call of trusting in God's sovereign rule over our lives. As you read the stories that follow, my hope is that you and your children will grow in gratitude so that giving "thanks in all circumstances" (1 Thessalonians 5:18, NIV) will become a defining attribute of your family.

Barbara Rainey

GRATITUDE

MEMORY VERSE

In everything give thanks; for this is God's will for you in Christ Jesus. —1 THESSALONIANS 5:18

can fleas be from God?

giving thanks for discomfort

Ravensbrück wasn't a place anyone wanted to be. Each day it was the scene of cruel suffering, sickness, and death. Located fifty miles north of Berlin, Germany, it had been established as a prison camp for women in 1938 by members of Adolf Hitler's army.

Corrie and Betsie ten Boom, along with their eighty-year-old father and two other family members, had been arrested for the crime of hiding Jews from the Nazi* soldiers. In 1944 Corrie and Betsie were unloaded at Ravensbrück with thousands of other women. Yet not even the horrific conditions of the camp or the threats of punishment could stop these two godly women from loving the persecuted Jewish people. At the risk of death, they tended the sick and injured, careful to avoid being seen by the prison guards, and secretly led times of Scripture reading and prayer.

Then the two sisters were moved to Barracks 28, where the living conditions were as bad as any in the camp. The backed-up plumbing filled the air with a sickening stench. The beds were actually long rows of crude wooden platforms stacked three high. What little straw covered the

> In everything give thanks; for this is God's will for you in Christ Jesus.
> —1 THESSALONIANS 5:18

> *"Betsie, how can we live in such a place?"*

beds was dirty and scratchy, and, of course, there were no sheets, blankets, or pillows.

After being directed to their beds, Corrie and Betsie crawled over the smelly straw and lay down to rest. Then . . .

"Fleas!" Corrie cried. "Betsie, the place is swarming with them! How can we live in such a place!"

"Show us how, Lord," Betsie prayed.

Suddenly she exclaimed, "Corrie, He's given us the answer! In the Bible this morning . . . Read that part again!"

Corrie made sure no guard was in sight, then drew the Bible from its pouch. "It was in First Thessalonians," she said. "'See that none of you repays evil for evil, but always seek to

---

*See Reference Points on page 33 for descriptions of certain terms, titles, and historical figures.

do good to one another . . . Rejoice always, pray constantly, give thanks in all circumstances; for this is the will of God in Christ Jesus—'"

"That's His answer," said Betsie. "'Give thanks in all circumstances!' We can thank God for every single thing about this barracks!"

"Such as?" Corrie said.

"Such as being assigned here together . . . and for what you're holding in your hands."

Corrie looked down at the Bible. "Yes! Thank You, Lord."

"Yes," said Betsie. "Thank You that we're packed so close, that many more will hear about You! . . . And thank You for the fleas."

This was too much. "Betsie, there's no way God can make me grateful for a flea."

"'Give thanks in all circumstances.'" Betsie quoted. "It doesn't say, 'in pleasant circumstances.' Fleas are part of this place where God has put us."

So we stood between piers of bunks and gave thanks for fleas. But I was sure Betsie was wrong.[1]

Weeks later, however, God gave Corrie the answer to her question about fleas when Betsie told her:

We've never understood why we had so much freedom in the big room. Well—I've found out. This afternoon some women asked for a supervisor to come settle a dispute, but she refused. Even the guards wouldn't come. And you know why? Because of the fleas! The supervisor said, "That place is crawling with fleas!"[2]

In any other barracks, it would have been very difficult to read the forbidden Bible without being discovered by the guards. But God provided protection by way of fleas.

Are we grateful for the daily comforts we enjoy that these women prisoners didn't have? Do we give thanks even for the nuisances God allows in our lives? We may never learn the reason for our suffering, as Betsie and Corrie did, but we can know that God is always caring for us no matter how difficult our circumstances may be.

giving thanks for discomfort

What unpleasant or uncomfortable circumstances in your life can you give thanks for, even though, like Corrie and Betsie, you can't see the good in them right now? Will you be bold enough to ask God to show you why he has allowed these difficulties in your life? He may not show you right away—or ever—but he is a loving Father who wants his children to ask.

what are we thankful for?   date

praying together with gratitude

Heavenly Father, you see where we live, and you understand the hardships that sometimes come into our lives. Even though trials are difficult, we know that you plan to use them to bring about good even if we never know why. We ask for the strength to bear each difficulty, the patience not to give up, and the faith to see your will accomplished in our lives. Help us to honor you by believing and to always give thanks in every circumstance.

Read more of Corrie and Betsie's story in the book *The Hiding Place* (Grand Rapids: Chosen Books, 1984). Consider reading it aloud as a family. It's appropriate for children ages twelve and older.

can you see it?
finding the good in the bad

An eight-year-old, whom we'll call Amy, wrote in her diary:

Today I forgot to brush my hair and my watch almost broke. My brother goes around the house screaming and bothering me. I can't not take anymore. I almost feel like running away, but I can't because I simple have no place to go. Darin is a pain at school. Mr. O'Neil picks Vern all the time. It has been a bad day. I'm glad nothing will be rong in heaven![1]

We all have bad days; sometimes we have several in a row. Often our bad days are simply full of nuisances like Amy's little brother, or a driver in front of us who is going so slowly we're late for an appointment, or the grocery store running out of the one item we need for dinner. The vacuum breaks, our favorite T-shirt gets lost, our cell phone keeps dropping calls, a neighbor

> Always giving thanks for all things in the name of our Lord Jesus Christ.
> —EPHESIANS 5:20

Are you willing to look for the good that God intends in something that may seem bad?

complains about where we put our trash can. It's pouring rain—again—and the kids are stuck in the house all day. Inconveniences and inconsiderate people can make for bad days.

But think for a moment. Is it possible that God is using that slow driver in front of you to protect you from a wreck? When you lose a valued possession, might God be teaching you contentment? When someone in your life is being difficult, could God be giving you an opportunity to pray and see what he will do? Proverbs 16:9 says, "The mind of man plans his way, but the LORD directs his steps." Are you willing to look for the good that God intends in something that may seem bad?

Matthew Henry was a Puritan preacher in the late 1600s. Like our friend Amy, he once wrote in his diary about something bad that happened to him. One day, while walking home in London, he was robbed by a couple of men who jumped him from the shadows of an alley. Being robbed is hardly an everyday nuisance; it's much more unsettling, a personal violation that can leave one

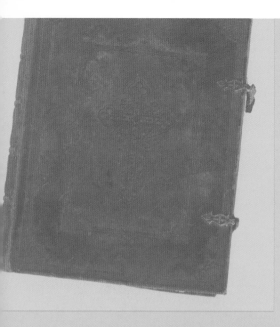

feeling vulnerable and frightened. Reverend Henry probably felt those things, but what he wrote that night is very instructive:

> I thank Thee, first, because I was never robbed before; second, because altho' they took my belongings, they did not take my life; third, altho' they took everything I had, it was not much; and fourth, because it was I who was robbed and not I who robbed![2]

What a great perspective on a difficult situation!

Matthew Henry chose to look for the good that was hidden in the bad. And by doing so, he showed us how important it is to focus on the positive that God wants us to see in every situation in life. It's always there; we just have to choose to look for it.

When we give thanks, we're saying to God that he is good in all he orders for our lives. And we are filling our minds with the larger truth about our situation and about him, not just feeling sorry for ourselves that bad things have happened. Thanking God isn't a magic wand that makes everything perfect, but it does bring balance to our emotions so that we aren't overwhelmed with sadness or loneliness or unhappiness.

giving thanks for the good in the bad

What hard things have happened to you recently? Are you willing to look for the hidden good in them? Do as Matthew Henry did and write down what you can be thankful for in your hard situation.

what are we thankful for?	date

praying together with gratitude

Almighty and Dependable One, you never turn against us. Even when evil or harmful things happen, you are not to blame. You are good. Your ways are always right. And your righteousness will ultimately prevail. So, until you bring an end to all evil, we hide behind the high wall of your grace. Help us remember that we do not deserve your great kindnesses, but because of Jesus we are loved and have hope. Help us remember that you are aware of every step we take, every interaction we make, every turn in our path. You are the great "I AM," and we gladly submit to your kingship.

what would you do?
being thankful when you've been betrayed

(*Note:* This story may be too disturbing for younger children. Please read it first and then decide if your children are mature enough for the subject matter.)

In the Bible, the story of Jesus' death by crucifixion is told in great detail. One important lesson Jesus taught during his capture and imprisonment was that he didn't try to get even with those who hurt him. He didn't try to correct his accusers when they made up lies about him. He was willing to wait and let God his Father make everything right in the future: "'Vengeance is mine, I will repay,' says the Lord" (Romans 12:19).

Since Jesus died two thousand years ago, thousands of men, women, and children have been martyred (being martyred means to be killed for your faith). Two Chinese girls followed Jesus' example when they were put in prison and sentenced to be killed simply because they were Christians. Here's what happened:

Love . . . does not take into account a wrong suffered.

—1 CORINTHIANS 13:4–5

"May God reward you . . . We die with gratitude."

The two Christian girls waited in the Chinese prison yard for the announced execution. A fellow prisoner who watched from his prison cell described their faces as pale but beautiful beyond belief; infinitely sad but sweet. Humanly speaking, they were fearful. But Chiu-Chin-Hsiu and Ho-Hsiu-Tzu had decided to submit to death without renouncing their faith.

Flanked by renegade guards, the executioner came with a revolver in his hand. It was their own pastor! He had been sentenced to die with the two girls. But, as on many other occasions in church history, the persecutors worked on him, tempting him. They promised to release him if he would shoot the girls. He accepted.

The girls whispered to each other, then bowed respectfully before their pastor. One of them said, "Before you shoot us, we wish to thank you heartily for what you have meant to us. You baptized us, you taught us the ways of eternal life, you gave us holy communion with the same hand in which you now hold the gun.

"You also taught us that Christians are sometimes weak and commit terrible sins, but they can be forgiven again. When you regret what you are about to do to us, do not despair like Judas, but repent like Peter. God bless you, and remember that our last thought was not one of indignation against your failures. Everyone passes through hours of darkness.

"May God reward you for all the good you have done to us. We die with gratitude."[1]

The pastor's heart had been so hardened that he did the unthinkable: He shot the girls. And soon afterward, he himself was shot by the prison guards.

We who live in America can hardly understand how this could happen. We live in a country that has given us many great freedoms, but for centuries there have been countries with rulers and dictators who have not allowed freedom of religion, freedom of speech, or freedom of the press. As a result of totalitarian rule, many people have been killed simply for what they believed. Sadly, there are still countries like this today.

What would you do if you were taken prisoner because you believe in Jesus? Could you be as courageous as these two young girls? How were they able to be grateful to the man who was about to kill them? And how did their response—in the face of betrayal and death—remind you of Jesus?

Even though you may not face anything like the persecution these girls faced, it's very likely that, at some time, you'll be betrayed by a friend. Jesus was betrayed by Judas Iscariot. The two Chinese girls were betrayed by their pastor. When a friend turns his or her back on you and does things that are hurtful, what should you do? Get even? Or give thanks? Jesus said in Matthew 5:44, "But I say to you, love your enemies and pray for those who persecute you." Giving thanks in prayer for those who hurt you is a strong weapon against becoming bitter, hateful, and intent on revenge.

giving thanks for our freedom

In the United States and in other free nations, each day we should give thanks for the freedoms we enjoy. As you think about this story, pray for those who are suffering persecution for their faith in Christ. Pray also for those who have betrayed or hurt you.

what are we thankful for?   date

praying together with gratitude

Keeper of Our Days, our lives belong to you. Thank you for the comfort that truth brings. Thank you that you go in front of us and behind—that we are never out of your sight. Keep us alert to the reality of your presence. Help us to be quick to call on you when we're in need, and make us eager to express our gratitude in everything.

An insightful book about the persecutions that Chinese Christians live with every day is the novel *Safely Home* by Randy Alcorn (Carol Stream, IL: Tyndale, 1991). It's a wonderful book for teens and adults to read as a family.

Blessed Assurance

FANNY J. CROSBY

1. Bless-ed as-sur-ance, Je-sus is mine! Oh, what a
2. Per - fect sub-mis-sion, per-fect de-light, Vi-sions of
3. Per - fect sub-mis-sion, all is at rest, I in my

glo-ry di-vine! Heir of sal-va-tion, pur-cha
burst on my sight: An-gels de-scend-ing bring fro
hap-py and blest: Watch-ing and wait-ing, look-in

can God still use me?
being thankful for handicaps

Helen Keller, born in 1880, became both blind and deaf before she reached her second birthday. For decades her life has been an inspiration to many of the power of determination to overcome significant challenges. She didn't allow herself to become a victim, feeling sorry for herself and demanding that others take care of her. Instead, she accepted her limitations and worked to overcome them.

Helen once said, "I thank God for my handicaps, for, through them, I have found myself, my work, and my God."[1] Throughout her life, she worked to improve the conditions of others who were blind, wrote many books, and received numerous awards and honors for her efforts.

Fanny Crosby was another woman who became blind early in life, the result of a doctor's error when she was just six weeks old. But her parents didn't seek revenge; they knew it wouldn't reverse the damage that had been done. They did, however, do all they could to help their daughter grow and learn and become independent. Fanny didn't let her condition limit

> For everything created by God is good.
> —1 TIMOTHY 4:4

> "It was the best thing that could have happened to me."

her. She climbed trees with other children and studied hard to learn as much as her siblings and friends.

Like Helen Keller, Fanny also said on many occasions that she was grateful for her blindness. "It was the best thing that could have happened to me . . . If I could meet [the doctor], I would tell him that he unwittingly did me the greatest favor in the world."[2] Because she couldn't see, Fanny developed other assets, such as a keen memory and a strong ability to concentrate. Her hearing was also more sensitive, as was her spiritual attentiveness to people's hearts. She believed that her lack of sight made her a better speaker because her blindness created a bond of sympathy with her audience that made them more receptive to hearing the truths of the Bible that she talked about so often. Fanny became most famous for writing thousands of hymns and songs for the church, many of which are still sung today.

Handicaps are rarely met with rejoicing; instead, they are typically met with sadness and fear.

This is understandable because they generally signal the loss of something. Many in our world are afflicted with physical conditions like diabetes, crippled legs or arms, epilepsy, cleft palates, and many other deformities and diseases. Others are handicapped emotionally by the loss of a loved one through death or divorce.

There are less obvious handicaps that are even more common, such as speech impediments, poor eyesight, lack of coordination, dyslexia, or other learning disabilities. Our personal insecurities, such as being shy or afraid of heights or public speaking, are limitations that can hold us back from accomplishing what we'd like to do. Even something that can't be overcome, such as our height or some other physical characteristic, can be seen as a limitation.

The bottom line is that we're all born with limitations, whether severe or minor. We live in a broken and imperfect world that is filled with people who are also broken and imperfect. None of us uses our intelligence to its full potential. None of us has the eyesight or the hearing or the perception or the physical, emotional, or intellectual ability that we'll one day have when God makes "all things new" (Revelation 21:5), as he promises those who belong to him.

Handicaps are difficult to deal with, but how we respond to the difficulties in our lives is more important than the handicaps themselves. We need to do all we can to correct what can be repaired and changed with God's help. And we need to pray for wisdom in how to live with the limitations we have. As Helen Keller and Fanny Crosby discovered, there is great joy to be found in serving others from the place of our limitations. God can and wants to use us the way we are for his purposes.

giving thanks for our limitations

To know that all of us are flawed and broken can be a great relief. We so often look at others and assume that everything is perfect, or at least close to perfect. But it's not. All of us have handicaps, and it would be a good demonstration of faith to name them and then give thanks for those "gifts" in your life.

what are we thankful for?   date

_____   _____

_____   _____

_____   _____

_____   _____

_____   _____

praying together with gratitude

Holiest One, how wonderful it is to be called a friend of God. You know we are broken and wounded, and yet you still want us. You feel great compassion for us, and as our Father, you long to help us. Thank you for never pulling away or leaving us to face life on our own. Thank you for being a friend who is always near. You hear our loudest cries and our softest whimpers. You even understand our silence. Thank you for providing help for your children in limitless ways. Help us to see your hand at work and to always say thank you.

does God really know what's going on?

being thankful for providence

William Bradford, the governor of the Plymouth Colony in New England, suffered great loss during his childhood. When he was sixteen months old, his father died, and he never knew the man for whom he was named. At the age of four, after his mother remarried, young William was sent to live with his grandfather for unknown reasons. When his grandfather died two years later, he was sent back to live with his mother and stepfather. The greatest loss of his young life occurred a year later when his mother also died.

The Bible tells us that God "will neither slumber nor sleep" (Psalm 121:4), so we must believe that he was fully aware of all that was going on in William's life. What was God doing? Why did he allow such pain to fall on one so young and alone?

After moving to his fourth home in seven years, William found himself living with two uncles in another village in England. They were delighted to have another worker for their farm. But William's trials weren't over. He soon became sick and didn't recover quickly.

Having been predestined according to His purpose who works all things after the counsel of His will. —EPHESIANS 1:11

Why did God allow such pain to fall on one so young and alone?

During his long illness, we finally see a glimmer of hope that God was indeed in control. Because William was unable to do manual labor, he was allowed to learn to read and write— skills that very few commoners were able to acquire in the 1600s. William likely received his education from a local minister. Though his sickness left him frail and weak, by the age of twelve, he had read many books from the pastor's library, which of course included the Bible and other books such as *Foxe's Book of Martyrs*. God's providence—that he was providing for William's training and preparing him for future use—is clear to us now, though it wasn't so obvious at the time.

William's Bible reading drew him to God but also left him with questions. As a teenager, he was invited by a friend to attend another church in a nearby town. It was, however, a controversial church that was viewed as opposing the Queen of England. This church believed in teaching the true Word of God as man's authority.

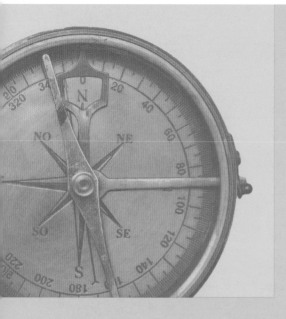

In spite of his uncles' strong objections, William chose to walk many miles each Sunday to attend this church. There he met Mr. Brewster, who became like a father to William, mentoring him in the faith and answering his questions about God. Years later in 1620, Mr. Brewster joined William Bradford on the journey to the New World aboard the *Mayflower*.[1]

God allowed William Bradford to endure many trials throughout his life because, in his providence, he was preparing William for his future calling. That calling included leading the colonists of Plymouth as they journeyed over the Atlantic to the New World, and then serving as their governor for more than thirty years.

In Jeremiah 29:11 God says, "I know the plans that I have for you." God wanted William to learn to read and write, as well as to think and pray, so that he could follow in the path God had prepared beforehand.

The following prayer echoes the ones William Bradford and the Puritans who sailed on the *Mayflower* might have prayed. Some of the words sound different from those we use in our prayers today, but sometimes it's good to pray using someone else's words. This helps us think about God in different terms.

A Puritan Prayer

Heavenly Father,

I believe thee,

I accept thy Word,

I submit to thy will,

I rely on thy promises,

I trust thy providence.

Thy providence has set the bounds of my habitation,

and wisely administers all my affairs.

Help me to see your providence in all that concerns me

And may I ever give you thanks.

Amen.[2]

giving thanks for providence

Providence has been described as "the evidence that God has not left this planet alone in the vast universe or forgotten for a moment the human situation. God visits, touches, communicates, controls, and intervenes, coming before and between man and his needs. Providence is the ground for thankfulness."[3]

Can you believe that God is providentially working in your life and your circumstances? Give thanks today for what he has allowed in your life that may not make sense to you right now. God isn't asleep. He has a plan for your life. Will you choose to believe that he is at work?

what are we thankful for?   date

praying together with gratitude

All-wise Creator, your providence has determined my family, my place on this earth, my gifts and abilities. You wisely supervise all my concerns, my activities, my life experiences. Thank you for uniquely designing and making each person. Help us remember, when we acknowledge you and ask for your purposes to be accomplished in our lives, that you lead and guide us and give us great joy in living. You are glorious!

is there a way out?
being thankful for deliverance

WILSON CHINN, a Branded Slave from Louisiana.
Also exhibiting Instruments of Torture
used to punish Slaves.

Photographed by KIMBALL, 477 Broadway, N. Y.

Entered according to Act of Congress, in the year 1863, by
GEO. H. HANKS, in the Clerk's Office of the United States for
the Southern District of New-York.

$200 Reward.

RANAWAY from the subscriber, on the night of Thursday, the 30th of Sepember,

FIVE NEGRO SLAVES,

To-wit: one Negro man, his wife, and three children.

The man is a black negro, full height, very erect, his face a little thin. He is about forty years of age, and calls himself *Washington Reed*, and is known by the name of Washington. He is probably well dressed, possibly takes with him an ivory headed cane, and is of good address. Several of his teeth are gone.

Mary, his wife, is about thirty years of age, a bright mulatto woman, and quite stout and strong.

The oldest of the children is a boy, of the name of FIELDING, twelve years of age, a dark mulatto, with heavy eyelids. He probably wore a new cloth cap.

MATILDA, the second child, is a girl, six years of age, rather a dark mulatto, but a bright and smart looking child.

MALCOLM, the youngest, is a boy, four years old, a lighter mulatto than the last, and about equally as bright. He probably also wore a cloth cap. If examined, he will be found to have a swelling at the navel.

Washington and Mary have lived at or near St. Louis, with the subscriber, for about 15 years.

It is supposed that they are making their way to Chicago, and that a white man accompanies them, that they will travel chiefly at night, and most probably in a covered wagon.

A reward of $150 will be paid for their apprehension, so that I can get them, if taken within one hundred miles of St. Louis, and $200 if taken beyond that, and secured so that I can get them, and other reasonable additional charges, if delivered to the subscriber, or to THOMAS ALLEN, Esq., at St. Louis, Mo. The above negroes, for the last few years, have been in possession of Thomas Allen, Esq., of St. Louis.

WM. RUSSELL.

ST. LOUIS, Oct. 1, 1847.

It was dark and time to move again. The woman leading the small group encouraged them to move quietly and quickly even though they were exhausted and hungry. After many hours of walking in the darkness, Harriet Tubman tiptoed silently to the farmhouse door and knocked. The door cracked open, and the man inside asked in a frightened voice, "Who is it?" When Harriet gave the password, "a friend with friends," the farmer told them to go away. He hurriedly explained that slave catchers had searched his house the day before, and he couldn't take the risk.

Stumbling back into the deep darkness of the woods, the runaway slaves crawled under bushes and piles of leaves to hide as dawn began to lighten the sky. As they fell asleep, their deliverer was praying intently to her heavenly Friend, asking him to lead them through the ever-present danger to safety. Harriet never slept but kept watch throughout the day and prayed without ceasing.

As night fell once again and the group prepared to move, they heard the voice of someone

> Call upon Me in the day of trouble; I shall rescue you, and you will honor Me.
> —PSALM 50:15

> As they fell asleep, their deliverer was praying intently to her heavenly Friend.

approaching. In fear, everyone retreated to their hiding places. But as the voice came nearer, Harriet heard the words, "My wagon stands in the barnyard across the way. The horse is in the stable. The harness hangs on a nail." The man continued walking, repeating these words until he was gone. When the night sky was completely dark, Harriet crept out of the woods and found the barn. Waiting there were all the things the man had mentioned, including blankets and baskets of food. God had provided for their needs and their deliverance.

As the runaway slaves were climbing into the wagon, they proclaimed, "Praise God! Thank you, Jesus!" over and over.[1] They knew without question that God is the One who saves and delivers. Giving thanks was their natural response.

There are countless stories of liberation in the Bible: God using Moses to deliver the Israelites from slavery in Egypt, Paul and Silas being released from prison, David being delivered from Saul and his enemies over and over, and Paul being saved from the venom of a snakebite. But

deliverance isn't just for slaves or for those who lived in biblical times. Every person needs to be delivered. Jesus said of himself, "[God] has sent me . . . to proclaim liberty to captives and freedom to prisoners" (Isaiah 61:1).

In what way are we captives? What makes us prisoners like the slaves Harriet Tubman rescued? The Bible teaches that all of us—men and women, boys and girls—are trapped by sin. We are born separated from God, and our selfishness and bad choices keep us captive. But God loved us so much that he sent his Son, Jesus, to pay the price to free us. When we give our lives to Jesus, he sets us free from our sin. We, like the slaves in this story, have much to give thanks for if Jesus has delivered us.

God also delivers his children in other ways. Some people have been delivered from sickness, some have been saved from accidents, some have been rescued from fires, and many have been set free from angry, hateful hearts toward others. God's greatest miracles are worked in the human heart.

Have you been delivered from the slavery of your sin? Have you let God deliver you from an angry heart and the desire to get even?

The wonderful hymn by John Newton says it so well:

> Amazing grace—
> how sweet the sound,
> that saved a wretch like me!
> I once was lost
> but now am found,
> was blind but now I see.[2]

giving thanks for deliverance

If everyone in your family has been set free by Jesus, then together give thanks for that most wonderful of all deliverances. If there are members of your family who don't yet know Jesus—a little brother or sister, a parent or grandparent, an aunt or uncle—then pray together for that person's deliverance. Thank God that he loves that person even more than you do.

Now think of other ways that God has delivered you or someone in your family, and thank him. Finally, ask God if there is anything else he wants to deliver you from—anger, bitterness, selfishness, getting even with those who hurt you, or other attitudes that aren't pleasing to him.

what are we thankful for?   date

praying together with gratitude

Heavenly Father, as your children we want to become more like you. Help us not just to receive your love but to freely give it away, not only to be partakers of your grace but dispensers of your grace to others as well. Grant us the courage not only to talk about you at church but also to speak boldly of the wonders of belonging to your forever family. Give us eyes to see those in need all around us, ears to hear the words of pain spoken by a friend, and a heart to act with compassion on behalf of strangers, orphans, the destitute, and the lonely. Help us, Father, to imitate you.

why does it hurt sometimes?

being thankful when there's no rescue

David Livingstone was a missionary to Africa. When he was twenty-seven years old, he traveled from England to South Africa with new ideas to teach the people of that continent about Jesus Christ. One of his ideas was to train African Christians to reach their own people with the gospel. Though this seems like common sense today, when Livingstone suggested it in the 1840s, he was ridiculed.

Raising his own money to begin building a mission station two hundred miles into the interior of Africa, David Livingstone wasn't afraid to go where no white missionaries had ever been. For three months he and an African teacher and several others built the mission station, which included a small house and another building for teaching the local villagers and treating their illnesses.

While they were working one day, someone came from a nearby village to report that lions were attacking their cattle. The villagers were frightened. "These must be devil lions," they said, "because ordinary lions don't attack during the day."

I have learned to be content in whatever circumstance I am.

—PHILIPPIANS 4:11

"These must be devil lions . . . ordinary lions don't attack during the day."

"Don't be afraid," said Livingstone. Interrupting the work on the mission buildings, he called Mebalwe, an African teacher, saying, "Come with me. If we shoot one, that will scare off the others."

Soon after they reached the cattle, a lion broke into one of the pens. Livingstone raised his gun and fired both barrels. The lion jerked back and roared. Quickly, Livingstone reloaded. Mebalwe yelled a warning. Livingstone looked up just as the lion sprang. It caught Livingstone's shoulder in its huge jaws, crushing the bone. Both man and animal rolled in the dust. When the lion returned to its feet, it shook the missionary like a rag doll. Livingstone later recalled thinking, *"What part of me will he eat first?"*

Mebalwe raised his gun, fired, and missed. The lion immediately dropped Livingstone and charged the African teacher, clamping its teeth into the teacher's leg. A villager tried to spear the lion, but it turned and charged toward him. Then suddenly the lion fell dead as a bullet from

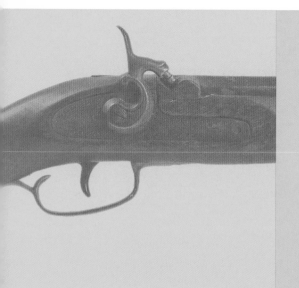

Livingstone's gun brought him down. The seriously injured missionary had managed to pick up his gun and shoot the lion a second time.

The other lions, watching and waiting for the kill, ran off and did not return. But Livingstone and Mebalwe needed medical attention. They were taken back to their mission station and then were transported to the mission headquarters on the coast, where they were treated for their injuries.

While there, David Livingstone wrote to his father in Scotland, praising and thanking God for saving him from great danger. Even though he wasn't delivered from the teeth of the lion, he was grateful he wasn't killed. He knew that God's hand had spared him.[1]

Sometimes God doesn't deliver us as we wish he would. Sometimes there are accidents, and people are hurt. Sometimes we get sick and suffer.

When Jesus died on the cross, it might have looked like God made a mistake. But we know that he was in control. And yet God didn't make Judas betray Jesus or stir up the crowd of men who demanded his death or tell the soldiers to mock and spit on Jesus. It was Satan, the devil, who was behind the evil things that happened to Jesus. Somehow, both the God of heaven and the devil of hell participated in the events that took place when Jesus died on the cross.

The same is true of David Livingstone. God didn't make the lion charge the cattle and the people. But he did keep the men alive and healed them with the help of skilled medical workers at the mission headquarters.

It's a great mystery to us how God works, as well as how much harm the devil can do. But our job is to thank God in everything because we know that he loves us and can bring good out of anything that happens to us, whether by delivering us from trouble or allowing us to suffer pain as David Livingstone did. As long as we're alive, may we be found praising and thanking God for all that happens in our lives.

giving thanks when there's no rescue in sight

Why do you think God didn't stop the lions from attacking? What do you think the villagers thought and said to each other about the missionaries who came to their rescue? Even though there was no miracle, did God make himself known to the villagers?

When you've been in a hard place, attacked by someone's words or actions or hurt physically by something, did you remember to thank God? It's not easy to do, but we can choose to give thanks in all things, even when God doesn't deliver us as we wish he would. God is always in control!

what are we thankful for?   date

praying together with gratitude

Eternal Savior, you are our Rescuer and Deliverer. Salvation comes from you alone, and we thank you for the freedom you offer us through your Son, Jesus Christ. When you save us, we are safe forever! Thank you for rescuing us through Jesus. And now for this day, we ask that you help us see how good your will is, even when it isn't what we desire. We will ask you for deliverance, as you would want us to, but if you don't rescue us today, then give us the humility to trust you, the One who is all wise, always acting with goodness on our behalf. And may we remember to express a heart of faith by giving you thanks, today and always.

WHAT WE ARE THANKFUL FOR

date

Keep looking for opportunities to thank your Father in heaven. When you see God at work around you, record your experience here and share it with your family. Keep these reminders as an offering of thanksgiving to God.

date

REFERENCE POINTS

DAY ONE: **Nazis** were led by Adolf Hitler in an aggressive war to take over Europe. They wanted to make the white race superior, seeking to remove Jews, people with disabilities, and many others.

Barracks are a group of buildings for housing or sleeping in a military facility—or as in the case of Ravensbrück, a concentration camp.

DAY TWO: The **Puritans** were a group of English-speaking Christians in the sixteenth and seventeenth centuries who disagreed with the Church of England. They worked together to purify themselves as well as England's morality, religion, and society. Escaping persecution from the church and the king, some Puritans risked their lives to settle in New England.

DAY FIVE: During the first winter in the **Plymouth Colony**, disease, lack of shelter from the harsh New England winter, and other conditions claimed the lives of 45 of the 102 Pilgrims who had arrived in the New World on the *Mayflower*.

DAY SIX: **Harriet Tubman** was a Christian who, following her own escape from slavery in 1849, led more than seventy slaves to freedom along the Underground Railroad.

The **Underground Railroad** was a secret web of routes and safe houses strung across the United States in the 1800s, helping thousands of enslaved African Americans in the South escape to the "free" northern states and Canada.

DAY SEVEN: **David Livingstone** was a Christian missionary and also became famous for exploring Africa. He died of malaria and dysentery, breathing his last while kneeling in prayer at his bedside. His missionary travels and exploration made him a national hero in Britain after his death and led to several major African missionary initiatives.

notes

Day 1

1. Adapted from Corrie ten Boom and John and Elizabeth Sherrill, *The Hiding Place* (Grand Rapids: Chosen Books, 1984), 180–81.
2. Ibid., 189–90.

Day 2

1. Margie Haack, "Thanksgiving Leftovers," *WORLD* 12, no. 28 (November 29, 1997), www.worldmag.com/articles/1420 (accessed August 27, 2010).
2. Matthew Henry, quoted in Haack, "Thanksgiving Leftovers."

Day 3

1. dc Talk and the Voice of the Martyrs, *Jesus Freaks: Stories of Those Who Stood for Jesus* (Tulsa, OK: Albury Publishing, 1999), 109–110.

Day 4

1. William J. Federer, *America's God and Country Encyclopedia of Quotations* (St. Louis: Amerisearch, 1994), 342–43.
2. Bonnie C. Harvey, *Fanny Crosby: Gospel Hymn Writer* (Minneapolis: Bethany House, 1999), 134–35.

Day 5

1. Information taken from Gary D. Schmidt, *William Bradford: Plymouth's Faithful Pilgrim* (Grand Rapids: Eerdmans Books for Young Readers, 1999).
2. Adapted from Arthur Bennett, *The Valley of Vision: A Collection of Puritan Prayers and Devotions* (Carlisle, PA: Banner of Truth Trust, 1975), 296.
3. Walter A. Elwell, ed., *Baker Encyclopedia of the Bible* (Grand Rapids: Baker, 1988), 2:1791.

Day 6

1. Adapted from Dave and Neta Jackson, *Heroes in Black History: True Stories from the Lives of Christian Heroes* (Bloomington, MN: Bethany House, 2008), 17–18.
2. John Newton, "Amazing Grace," 1779, public domain.

Day 7

1. Dave and Neta Jackson, *Hero Tales: A Family Treasury of True Stories from the Lives of Christian Heroes* (Bloomington, MN: Bethany House, 1996), 59–60.

photo credits

FRONT COVER

Young Helen Keller—http://commons.
wikimedia.org/wiki/Category:Helen_
Keller

Seven native children—Frank and Frances
Carpenter Collection, Library of
Congress

The First Thanksgiving—1621 / J.L.G.
Ferris, Library of Congress

Young crying woman—©iStockphoto.
com (Rudyanto Wijaya)

BACK COVER

Corrie ten Boom—Courtesy of the Corrie
ten Boom Foundation

$200.00 Reward poster—1847, Library of
Congress

Two young women—©Gary Friedman,
www.friedmanarchives.com

Lion—©iStockphoto.com
(Peter Malsbury)

PAGE VI

Boy releasing dove—©iStockphoto.com
(Andriy Petrenko)

PAGE 2

Corrie ten Boom—Courtesy of the Corrie
ten Boom Foundation

Forced labor interior—Used by
permission of The Collections of the
Ravensbrück/Brandenburg Memorials
Foundation

Female prisoners at forced labor
digging trenches at the Ravensbrük
concentration camp—Used by
permission of the U.S. Holocaust
Memorial Museum, courtesy of
Lydia Chagoll. The views or opinions
expressed in this book and the context
in which the images are used do not
necessarily reflect the views or policy of,
nor imply approval or endorsement by,
the U.S. Holocaust Memorial Museum,
www.ushmm.org

Female prisoners by railroad track—Used
by permission of the U.S. Holocaust
Memorial Museum. The views or
opinions expressed in this book and
the context in which the images are
used do not necessarily reflect the views
or policy of, nor imply approval or
endorsement by, the U.S. Holocaust
Memorial Museum, www.ushmm.org

PAGE 4

Tin cup—©iStockphoto.com
(Dan Van Oss)

PAGE 6

Matthew Henry—http://en.wikipedia.org/
wiki/Matthew_Henry

Old books—©Per Christensen/
Dreamstime.com

England street scene—MAYSON
BEETON COLLECTION, "Cheapside"
London engraving by Anonymous
1813, Copyright © English Heritage
Photo Library

Money wallet—©iStockphoto
(Lydia Neeleman)

Coins—©iStockphoto (Ilbusca)

PAGE 8

Old Bible—©iStockphoto.com
(Anssi Ruuska)

PAGE 10

Soldier—©Gary Friedman, www.
friedmanarchives.com

Two young women—©Gary Friedman,
www.friedmanarchives.com

The Great Wall—© Miao/Dreamstime.
com

Young crying woman—©iStockphoto.
com (Rudyanto Wijaya)

PAGE 12

Handcuffs—©iStockphoto.com
(Maxim Lysenko)

PAGE 14

Young Helen Keller—http://commons.
wikimedia.org/wiki/Category: Helen_
Keller

"Blessed Assurance"—from the Baptist
Hymnal ©1956, used by permission of
LifeWay Publishers

Helen Keller with Anne Sullivan—http://
commons.wikimedia.org/wiki/
Category: Helen_Keller

Fanny Crosby—The New York Institute
for Special Education, http://www.
nyise.org/fanny/words.html

PAGE 16

Glasses—©iStockphoto.com
(Richard Cano)

PAGE 18

William Bradford statue—photo by
Barbara Rainey

Church—©iStockphoto.com
(Karl Kehm)

The First Thanksgiving—1621 / J.L.G.
Ferris, Library of Congress

Mayflower Approaching Land—Date
unknown, Library of Congress

PAGE 20

Compass—©iStockphoto.com
(Jose Gutierrez)

PAGE 22

Hariett Tubman—H. B. Lindsley,
photographer, Library of
Congress

Group of contrabands—James F. Gibson,
photographer, Library of Congress

$200.00 Reward poster—1847, Library of
Congress

Wilson Chinn—c1863, Library of
Congress

PAGE 24

Wheel—©iStockphoto.com
(MBPhoto)

PAGE 26

David Livingstone—New York: Johnson,
Fry & Co. Publishers, c1872, Library of
Congress

Map of Africa—Courtesy of George
Karakehian and Art Source
International

Seven native children—Frank and Frances
Carpenter Collection, Library of
Congress

Lion—©iStockphoto.com
(Peter Malsbury)

PAGE 28

Rifle—©iStockphoto.com
(Blaney photo)

PAGE 37

Barbara Rainey—J. E. Stover
Photography, Inc.

A LETTER FROM THE AUTHOR

Dear Reader,

My husband and I had six children in ten years. The wide range of their ages and personalities made leading our children in any kind of home-centered spiritual direction a daunting task. So when a parent asks me how to encourage a fifteen-year-old in his faith while not ignoring the childlike questions of his five-year-old sister, I understand the predicament.

Where can a parent find stories and learning activities that are relevant to all ages? That was my dilemma; I could find no resources for a family like mine. I found lots of stories and songs for preschoolers and devotionals for teens, but nothing that would appeal to all of my children *together*.

What I did discover was that the best and easiest vehicle for transferring truth to my children was through stories. Whatever success we might have achieved in spiritually training our family came mostly through shared stories of faith, both our own stories and those of others. From that experience was born my dream to create a resource to help moms and dads who want to be instrumental in guiding their children toward God.

Parents need something that works, something that is easy, something that requires no preparation. These seven stories make that possible. And unlike most devotional books that feature different themes with each day's reading, this resource focuses on one character quality that all parents want to develop in their children—gratitude. By reinforcing this one topic, my hope is that you and your family will experience increased expressions of gratitude and a greater inclination to practice thanksgiving each and every day.

Thanks for using this short family devotional. I pray that you and your children will grow in gratitude as you are inspired by the great faith of these men and women whose stories I've shared.

Barbara Rainey

P.S. I'd love to hear from you as you use this resource with your family. I hope to create more daily stories for families on other character qualities, such as love, generosity, sacrifice, and forgiveness. I need your help in making these devotionals as user friendly and helpful as possible, so please go online to shopFamilyLife.com/gratitude.html and give your feedback and suggestions.

ABOUT THE AUTHOR

Barbara Rainey is the mother of six adult children and the "Mimi" of sixteen grandchildren. She and her husband, Dennis, give leadership to FamilyLife, a ministry committed to helping marriages and families survive and thrive in our generation. Barbara has written several books, including *Thanksgiving: A Time to Remember, Barbara and Susan's Guide to the Empty Nest,* and *When Christmas Came.* The Raineys live in Little Rock, Arkansas.

You can read more from Barbara online at FamilyLifeMomblog.com.

ABOUT THE SERIES

With captivating true stories to read as a family, these seven-day interactive devotionals from speaker and best-selling author Barbara Rainey saturate minds and hearts with memorable accounts and vivid illustrations of true heroes who made noble choices.

Each day also includes:

- A key Bible verse

- Questions to discuss together

- A suggested prayer

- A personal record of your family's character as it relates to these stories

Encounter real-life heroes right in your living room— and begin to grow together in character as a family.